Our Bodies

Our Stomachs

Charlotte Guillain

www.raintreepublishers.co.uk

Visit our website to find out more information about Raintree books.

To order:

☎ Phone 0845 6044371

🖹 Fax +44 (0) 1865 312263

✉ Email myorders@raintreepublishers.co.uk

Customers from outside the UK please telephone +44 1865 312262

Raintree is an imprint of Capstone Global Library Limited, a company incorporated in England and Wales having its registered office at 7 Pilgrim Street, London, EC4V 6LB – Registered company number: 6695582

Text © Capstone Global Library Limited 2010
First published in hardback in 2010
Paperback edition first published in 2011
The moral rights of the proprietor have been asserted.

Edited by Sian Smith, Laura Knowles, Nancy Dickmann, and Rebecca Rissman
Designed by Joanna Hinton-Malivoire
Original Illustrations © Capstone Global Library Ltd. 2010
Illustrated by Tony Wilson
Picture research by Ruth Blair and Mica Brancic
Production by Duncan Gilbert and Victoria Fitzgerald
Originated by Capstone Global Library Ltd
Printed and bound in China by South China Printing Company L

ISBN 978 0 431 19506 3 (hardback)
14 13 12 11 10
10 9 8 7 6 5 4 3 2 1

ISBN 978 0 431 19516 2 (paperback)
15 14 13 12 11
10 9 8 7 6 5 4 3 2 1

British Library Cataloguing in Publication Data
Guillain, Charlotte.
   Our stomachs. -- (Acorn. Our bodies)
   1. Stomach--Juvenile literature.
   I. Title II. Series
   612.3'2-dc22

Acknowledgements
We would like to thank the following for permission to reproduce photographs: © Capstone Global Library pp.**16**, **17** (Karon Dubke); Corbis p.**19** (© ROB & SAS); iStockphoto pp.**18** (© Rob Friedman), **20** (© Elena Elisseeva); Photolibrary pp.**4** (© Goodshoot), **5** (© Banana Stock), **8** (© Fancy), **9** (© 4x5 Coll-Paul Simcock/Superstock), **10** (© Stockbyte), **21** (© Brand X Pictures), **22** (© Banana Stock); Science Photo Library p.**12** (© Alfred Pasieka); Shutterstock pp.**13** (© Stephen Mcsweeny), **14** (© NatashaBo).

Front cover photograph of a girl picking an apple reproduced with permission of Corbis (© Rolf Brenner). Back cover photograph reproduced with permission of Photolibrary (© Stockbyte).

Contents

Body parts

Our bodies have many parts.

skin

arm

hand

leg

foot

Our bodies have parts on the outside.

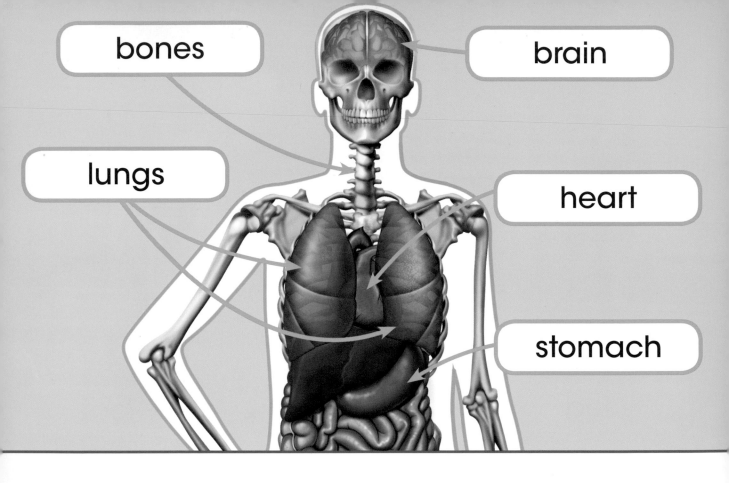

bones

brain

lungs

heart

stomach

Our bodies have parts on the inside.

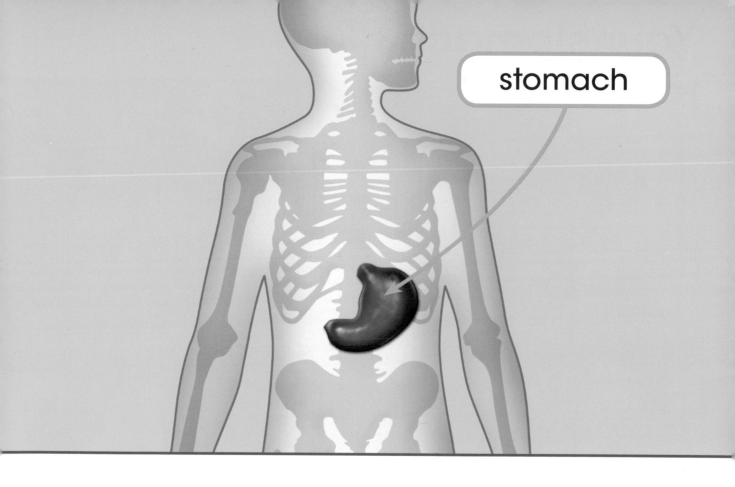

stomach

Your stomach is inside your body.

Your stomach

You cannot see your stomach.

tummy

Your stomach is inside your tummy.

Eating

mouth

You eat with your mouth.

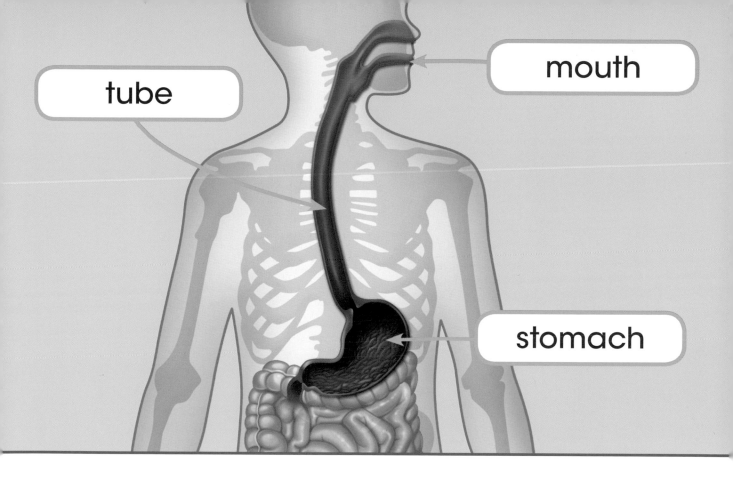

tube

mouth

stomach

A tube goes from your mouth to your stomach.

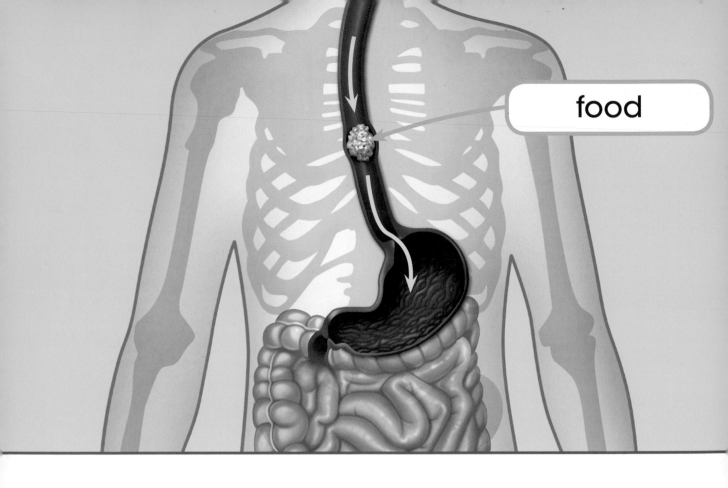

food

Food goes into your stomach.

Drinks go into your stomach, too.

Your stomach holds food like
a bag.

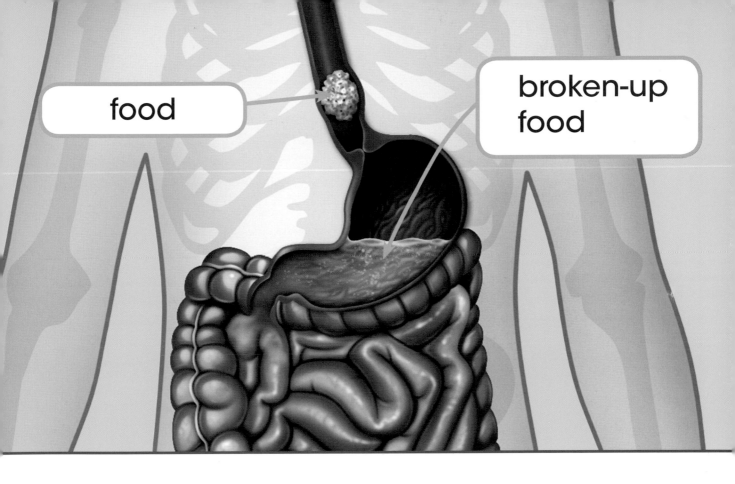

food

broken-up
food

Your stomach breaks up the food.

Full and empty

You can feel when your stomach is full.

Sometimes your stomach hurts when it is full.

You can feel when your stomach
is empty.

Sometimes your stomach makes
sounds when it is empty.

Staying healthy

You can drink a lot of water to help your stomach.

You can eat healthy food to help your stomach.

Quiz

Where in your body is
your stomach?

Answer on page 24

Picture glossary

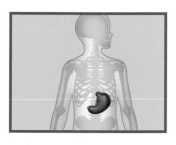

stomach part of your body inside your tummy. Your stomach breaks food into tiny bits so that your body can use it.

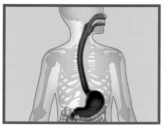

tube a long, thin pipe like a hose. Things can move along inside tubes because they have an empty space in the middle.

Index

Answer to quiz on page 22: Your stomach is inside your tummy.

Notes to parents and teachers

Before reading

Ask the children to name the parts of their body they can see on the outside. Then ask them what parts of their body are inside. Make a list of them together and see if the children know what each body part does, for example, they need their lungs to breathe. Discuss where their stomach is and see if anyone knows what our stomachs do.

After reading

• Read *The Very Hungry Caterpillar* together. Ask the children why the caterpillar had a stomach ache. How do they feel when they eat too much food?

• Put the children into groups and give each group a balloon and a funnel. Tell them that the flat balloon is like their stomachs when they are empty. Then ask them to use the funnel to slowly pour water into the balloon. Discuss how the balloon is stretching in the same way our stomachs stretch when we eat and drink.